INSIDE VB.NET

IDE DRIVEN CODE USING DAO WITH ISAMS

Richard Thomas Edwards

CONTENTS

Introduction

The way I see it, you will buy this book for the code

Certainly not for my good looks or my fantastic writing style!

You are here for one reason and one reason only. You are here for the source code.

If you are not, if you're here in search of a feeding trough of cerebral renditions on just how smart I am, and you aren't. Leave now! I'm sure you will find a 300-page book filled with all the technical jargon your heart desires.

For the rest of you, welcome aboard!

What you are about to see

If you have read any of my other books, you know I really don't have long winded introductions. I hope to not disappoint here. However, I do have something to say.

After this chapter, you will be inside one very large and powerful module that you can call from the form on load Event. The idea is and was to separate the necessary parts of the code into a source that is easy to use and call.

The purpose of doing this code this way is to be able to make the routines simple enough that I can take them and use them for literally almost every way possible. So, you're going to see the same routines driving the same IDE Controls in almost the same exact way.

If this offends anyone, my deepest apologies. There is only on way to write these routines, so they correctly render in the VB.Net IDE and that is that.

The Module starts with this:

```
Imports DAO
Module Module1
```

And ends with this:

```
End Module
```

I am are going chapter break at the top of a routine to signal that a new rendering is starting and at the end of it to show you how to use the routine.

Let's get started!

The initialization code
Making the complex, simple

The initialization code needed to create the recordset:

```
Public rs As Recordset
Public ds As System.Data.DataSet
Public dt As System.Data.DataTable
Public dv As System.Data.DataView


    Public Sub Open_DAO_Recordset_Using_DBEngine(ByVal strDriver
As String, ByVal strQuery As String)

        Dim DBEngine As New DAO.DBEngine
        Dim ws As Workspace =
DBEngine.CreateWorkspace("myODBCWorkspace", "", "",
DAO.WorkspaceTypeEnum.dbUseODBC)
        Dim db As Database = ws.OpenDatabase("", False, False,
strDriver)
        rs = db.OpenRecordset(strQuery,
RecordsetTypeEnum.dbOpenDynaset)
        rs.MoveLast()
        rs.MoveFirst()

    End Sub
```

Since this is short and to the point, we'll be doing what is needed to make the call here. You need to know where the Database is located and what table you want to use:

```
Imports DAO
Imports System.Xml
Public Class Form1
```

```
Private Sub Form1_Load(ByVal sender As System.Object, ByVal e As
System.EventArgs) Handles MyBase.Load

    Module1.Open_DAO_Recordset_Using_DBEngine("G:\nwind.mdb", Products")

End Sub

End Class
```

Notice that the module has made the rs, ds, dt and dv objects public so that once they are initialized, you can use them anywhere along the way.

Creating the DataSet from DAO

Below is the code logic needed to create the DataSet in various orientations:

```
Public Sub Create_DataSet_using_DAO_Recordset_Using_DBEngine(ByVal
Orientation As String)

    ds = New System.Data.DataSet
    dt = New System.Data.DataTable
    ds.Tables.Add(dt)


    Select Case Orientation


        Case "Multi Line Horizontal"

            For x As Integer = 0 To rs.Fields.Count - 1
                ds.Tables(0).Columns.Add(rs.Fields(x).Name)
            Next

            For y As Integer = 0 To rs.RecordCount - 1
                Dim dRow As System.Data.DataRow = ds.Tables(0).NewRow
                For x As Integer = 0 To rs.Fields.Count - 1
                    dRow.Item(rs.Fields(x).Name) = rs.Fields(x).Value
                Next
                ds.Tables(0).Rows.Add(dRow)
                rs.MoveNext()
            Next
```

```vb
Case "Multi Line Vertical"


    ds.Tables(0).Columns.Add("Property Name")
    For y As Integer = 0 To rs.RecordCount - 1
        ds.Tables(0).Columns.Add("Row" & y)
    Next

    For x As Integer = 0 To rs.Fields.Count - 1
        Dim dRow As System.Data.DataRow = ds.Tables(0).NewRow
        dRow("Property Name") = rs.Fields(x).Name
        rs.MoveFirst()
        For y As Integer = 0 To rs.RecordCount - 1
            dRow("Row" & y) = rs.Fields(x).Value
            rs.MoveNext()
        Next
        ds.Tables(0).Rows.Add(dRow)
    Next

Case "Single Line Horizontal"

    For x As Integer = 0 To rs.Fields.Count - 1
        ds.Tables(0).Columns.Add(rs.Fields(x).Name)
    Next

    For y As Integer = 0 To rs.RecordCount - 1
        Dim dRow As System.Data.DataRow = ds.Tables(0).NewRow
        For x As Integer = 0 To rs.Fields.Count - 1
            dRow.Item(rs.Fields(x).Name) = rs.Fields(x).Value
        Next
        ds.Tables(0).Rows.Add(dRow)
        Exit For
    Next


Case "Single Line Vertical"

    ds.Tables(0).Columns.Add("Property Name")
```

```vb
    ds.Tables(0).Columns.Add("Property Value")

    For x As Integer = 0 To rs.Fields.Count - 1
        Dim dRow As System.Data.DataRow = ds.Tables(0).NewRow
        dRow.Item("Property Name") = rs.Fields(x).Name
        dRow.Item("Property Value") = rs.Fields(x).Value
        ds.Tables(0).Rows.Add(dRow)
    Next

    End Select

End Sub
```

Why use the DataSet

Since DAO doesn't have a .Net DataAdapter like ADO has with the OleDbDataAdapter, we can't just fill a DataSet, DataTable or use the Default View directly, so we build them.

While all three routines designed to create them are remarkable similar. There are unique differences in them.

For example. The DataTable is used by all three routines. But the DataSet can be a collection of tables and the DataView is the DataTable and the DataSet Table collections default view.

To clarify, Dim dv as System.Data.DataView = ds.Tables().DefaultView is the same as, Dim dv as System.Data.DataView = dt.DefaultView

These routines are especially useful with WPF which will be in other books.

How to use it

```
Module1.Open_DAO_Recordset_Using_DBEngine("ODBC;Driver={Microsoft Access
Driver (*.mdb)};dbq=G:\nwind.mdb;", "Select * from [Products]")
```

```
Orientation:
```

```
Multi Line Horizontal
```

```
Module1.Create_DataSet_using_DAO_Recordset_Using_DBEngine("Multi Line
Horizontal")
```

```
Multi Line Vertical
```

```
Module1.Create_DataSet_using_DAO_Recordset_Using_DBEngine("Multi Line
Vertical")
```

Single Line Horizontal

```
Module1.Create_DataSet_using_DAO_Recordset_Using_DBEngine("Single Line
Horizontal")
```

Single Line Vertical

```
Module1.Create_DataSet_using_DAO_Recordset_Using_DBEngine("Single Line
Vertical")
```

Creating DataTable Code Using DAO

Chapter Subtitle

```
Public Sub Create_DataTable_using_DAO_Recordset_Using_DBEngine(ByVal
Orientation As String)


    dt = New System.Data.DataTable


    Select Case Orientation


        Case "Multi Line Horizontal"

            For x As Integer = 0 To rs.Fields.Count - 1
                dt.Columns.Add(rs.Fields(x).Name)
            Next

            For y As Integer = 0 To rs.RecordCount - 1
                Dim dRow As System.Data.DataRow = dt.NewRow
                For x As Integer = 0 To rs.Fields.Count - 1
```

```vbnet
            dRow.Item(rs.Fields(x).Name) = rs.Fields(x).Value
        Next
        dt.Rows.Add(dRow)
        rs.MoveNext()
    Next


Case "Multi Line Vertical"


    dt.Columns.Add("Property Name")
    For y As Integer = 0 To rs.RecordCount - 1
        dt.Columns.Add("Row" & y)
    Next

    For x As Integer = 0 To rs.Fields.Count - 1
        Dim dRow As System.Data.DataRow = dt.NewRow
        dRow("Property Name") = rs.Fields(x).Name
        rs.MoveFirst()
        For y As Integer = 0 To rs.RecordCount - 1
            dRow("Row" & y) = rs.Fields(x).Value
            rs.MoveNext()
        Next
        dt.Rows.Add(dRow)
    Next

Case "Single Line Horizontal"

    For x As Integer = 0 To rs.Fields.Count - 1
        dt.Columns.Add(rs.Fields(x).Name)
    Next

    For y As Integer = 0 To rs.RecordCount - 1
        Dim dRow As System.Data.DataRow = dt.NewRow
        For x As Integer = 0 To rs.Fields.Count - 1
            dRow.Item(rs.Fields(x).Name) = rs.Fields(x).Value
        Next
        dt.Rows.Add(dRow)
        Exit For
    Next
```

```
        Case "Single Line Vertical"

           dt.Columns.Add("Property Name")
           dt.Columns.Add("Property Value")

           For x As Integer = 0 To rs.Fields.Count - 1
              Dim dRow As System.Data.DataRow = dt.NewRow
              dRow.Item("Property Name") = rs.Fields(x).Name
              dRow.Item("Property Value") = rs.Fields(x).Value
              dt.Rows.Add(dRow)
           Next

        End Select

    End Sub
```

Why use the DataTable

While I have already covered the reasons why in the comments on using it with the DataSet, I'll Just say it is the core building block interface between other data collections and databinding on almost every other control in the .Net family of controls.

How to use it:

```
Module1.Open_DAO_Recordset_Using_DBEngine("ODBC;Driver={Microsoft Access
Driver (*.mdb)};dbq=G:\nwind.mdb;", "Select * from [Products]")
```

Orientation:

Multi Line Horizontal

```
Module1.Create_DataTable_using_DAO_Recordset_Using_DBEngine("Multi Line
Horizontal")
```

Multi Line Vertical

```
Module1.Create_DataTable_using_DAO_Recordset_Using_DBEngine("Multi Line
Vertical")
```

Single Line Horizontal


```
Module1.Create_DataTable_using_DAO_Recordset_Using_DBEngine("Single Line
Horizontal")
```

Single Line Vertical

```
Module1.Create_DataTable_using_DAO_Recordset_Using_DBEngine("Single Line
Vertical")
```

Creating the DataView code

Below is the code driven by DAO to create a DataView:

```
Public Sub Create_DataView_using_DAO_Recordset_Using_DBEngine(ByVal
Orientation As String)


    dt = New System.Data.DataTable
    dv = dt.DefaultView


    Select Case Orientation


      Case "Multi Line Horizontal"

        For x As Integer = 0 To rs.Fields.Count - 1
          dv.Table.Columns.Add(rs.Fields(x).Name)
        Next

        For y As Integer = 0 To rs.RecordCount - 1
          Dim dRow As System.Data.DataRow = dv.Table.NewRow
          For x As Integer = 0 To rs.Fields.Count - 1
            dRow.Item(rs.Fields(x).Name) = rs.Fields(x).Value
          Next
```

```vb
        dv.Table.Rows.Add(dRow)
        rs.MoveNext()
    Next


Case "Multi Line Vertical"


    dv.Table.Columns.Add("Property Name")
    For y As Integer = 0 To rs.RecordCount - 1
        dv.Table.Columns.Add("Row" & y)
    Next

    For x As Integer = 0 To rs.Fields.Count - 1
        Dim dRow As System.Data.DataRow = dv.Table.NewRow
        dRow("Property Name") = rs.Fields(x).Name
        rs.MoveFirst()
        For y As Integer = 0 To rs.RecordCount - 1
            dRow("Row" & y) = rs.Fields(x).Value
            rs.MoveNext()
        Next
        dv.Table.Rows.Add(dRow)
    Next

Case "Single Line Horizontal"

    For x As Integer = 0 To rs.Fields.Count - 1
        dv.Table.Columns.Add(rs.Fields(x).Name)
    Next

    For y As Integer = 0 To rs.RecordCount - 1
        Dim dRow As System.Data.DataRow = dv.Table.NewRow
        For x As Integer = 0 To rs.Fields.Count - 1
            dRow.Item(rs.Fields(x).Name) = rs.Fields(x).Value
        Next
        dv.Table.Rows.Add(dRow)
        Exit For
    Next
```

```
Case "Single Line Vertical"

    dv.Table.Columns.Add("Property Name")
    dv.Table.Columns.Add("Property Value")

    For x As Integer = 0 To rs.Fields.Count - 1
        Dim dRow As System.Data.DataRow = dv.Table.NewRow
        dRow.Item("Property Name") = rs.Fields(x).Name
        dRow.Item("Property Value") = rs.Fields(x).Value
        dv.Table.Rows.Add(dRow)
    Next

  End Select

End Sub
```

Why use the DataView

I think I've run out of reasons why this code is important. Let's just say it has its place in databinding on almost every other control in the .Net family of controls.

How to use it:

```
Module1.Open_DAO_Recordset_Using_DBEngine("ODBC;Driver={Microsoft Access
Driver (*.mdb)};dbq=G:\nwind.mdb;", "Select * from [Products]")
```

Orientation:

Multi Line Horizontal

```
Module1.Create_DataView_using_DAO_Recordset_Using_DBEngine("Multi Line
Horizontal")
```

Multi Line Vertical

```
Module1.Create_DataView_using_DAO_Recordset_Using_DBEngine("Multi Line
Vertical")
```

Single Line Horizontal

```
Module1.Create_DataView_using_DAO_Recordset_Using_DBEngine("Single Line
Horizontal")
```

Single Line Vertical

```
Module1.Create_DataView_using_DAO_Recordset_Using_DBEngine("Single Line
Vertical")
```

Binding The DataGridview to a DataSet, DataTable or DataView

Chapter Subtitle

```
Public Sub Bind_To_DataGridView(ByVal DG As DataGridView, ByVal dType As
String)

    Select Case dType

      Case "DataSet"

        DG.DataSource = ds.Tables(0)

      Case "DataTable"

        DG.DataSource = dt

      Case "DataView"

        DG.DataSource = dv
```

End Select

End Sub

Making the DataGridView DataSource work with the DataSet, DataTable or DataView

The code to make this work

```
Module1.Open_DAO_Recordset_Using_DBEngine("ODBC;Driver={Microsoft Access
Driver (*.mdb)};dbq=G:\nwind.mdb;", "Select * from [Products]")
```

For the DataSet:

Orientation:

Multi Line Horizontal

```
Module1.Create_DataSet_using_DAO_Recordset_Using_DBEngine("Multi Line
Horizontal")
```

Multi Line Vertical

Module1.**Create_DataSet_using_DAO_Recordset_Using_DBEngine**("Multi Line Vertical")

Single Line Horizontal

Module1.**Create_DataSet_using_DAO_Recordset_Using_DBEngine**("Single Line Horizontal")

Single Line Vertical

Module1.**Create_DataSet_using_DAO_Recordset_Using_DBEngine**("Single Line Vertical")

For the DataTable:

Orientation:

Multi Line Horizontal

Module1.**Create_DataTable_using_DAO_Recordset_Using_DBEngine**("Multi Line Horizontal")

Multi Line Vertical

Module1.**Create_DataTable_using_DAO_Recordset_Using_DBEngine**("Multi Line Vertical")

Single Line Horizontal

Module1.**Create_DataTable_using_DAO_Recordset_Using_DBEngine**("Single Line Horizontal")

Single Line Vertical

Module1.**Create_DataTable_using_DAO_Recordset_Using_DBEngine**("Single Line Vertical")

For the DataView:

Orientation:

Multi Line Horizontal

Module1.Create_DataView_using_DAO_Recordset_Using_DBEngine("Multi Line Horizontal")

Multi Line Vertical

Module1.Create_DataView_using_DAO_Recordset_Using_DBEngine("Multi Line Vertical")

Single Line Horizontal

Module1.Create_DataView_using_DAO_Recordset_Using_DBEngine("Single Line Horizontal")

Single Line Vertical

Module1.Create_DataView_using_DAO_Recordset_Using_DBEngine("Single Line Vertical")

Now, we call:

For the DataSet:

Bind_To_DataGridView(DataGridView1, DataSet)

For the DataTable:

Bind_To_DataGridView(DataGridView1, DataTable)

For the DataView:

Bind_To_DataGridView(DataGridView1, DataView)

Please Note:

This is the only time when you should call the create DataSet, DataTable, or DataView with anything but "Multi Line Horizontal". The routines aren't designed to enumerate through any other orientation.

Dynamically binding the DataGridView with DAO

Chapter Subtitle

```
Public Sub do_dao_code_for_dataGridView(ByVal DG As DataGridView, ByVal
Orientation As String)


    DG.Rows.Clear()
    DG.Columns.Clear()


    Select Case Orientation


        Case "Multi Line Horizontal"
```

```vb
    For x As Integer = 0 To rs.Fields.Count - 1
        DG.Columns.Add(rs.Fields(x).Name, rs.Fields(x).Name)
    Next

    For y As Integer = 0 To rs.RecordCount - 1
        DG.Rows.Add()
        For x As Integer = 0 To rs.Fields.Count - 1
            DG.Rows(y).Cells(x).Value = rs.Fields(x).Value
        Next
        rs.MoveNext()
    Next


Case "Multi Line Vertical"


    DG.Columns.Add("Property Name", "Property Name")
    For y As Integer = 0 To rs.RecordCount - 1
        DG.Columns.Add("Row" & y, "Row" & y)
    Next

    For x As Integer = 0 To rs.Fields.Count - 1
        DG.Rows.Add()
        DG.Rows(x).Cells(0).Value = rs.Fields(x).Name
        rs.MoveFirst()
        For y As Integer = 0 To rs.RecordCount - 1
            DG.Rows(x).Cells(y + 1).Value = rs.Fields(x).Value
            rs.MoveNext()
        Next
    Next

Case "Single Line Horizontal"


    For x As Integer = 0 To rs.Fields.Count - 1
        DG.Columns.Add(rs.Fields(x).Name, rs.Fields(x).Name)
    Next

    For y As Integer = 0 To rs.RecordCount - 1
        DG.Rows.Add()
```

```vb
            For x As Integer = 0 To rs.Fields.Count - 1
                DG.Rows(y).Cells(x).Value = rs.Fields(x).Value
            Next
            Exit For
        Next


        Case "Single Line Vertical"


            DG.Columns.Add("Property Name", "Property Name")
            DG.Columns.Add("Property Value", "Property Value")

            For x As Integer = 0 To rs.Fields.Count - 1
                DG.Rows.Add()
                DG.Rows(x).Cells(0).Value = rs.Fields(x).Name
                DG.Rows(x).Cells(1).Value = rs.Fields(x).Value
            Next

    End Select

End Sub
```

Making the DataGridview work using DAO

Okay, so here's the long and short version on how this works.

```
Module1.Open_DAO_Recordset_Using_DBEngine("ODBC;Driver={Microsoft Access
Driver (*.mdb)};dbq=G:\nwind.mdb;", "Select * from [Products]")
```

Orientation:

Multi Line Horizontal

```
Module1.do_dao_code_for_dataGridView(DataGridView1, "Multi Line
Horizontal")
```

Multi Line Vertical

```
Module1.do_dao_code_for_dataGridView(DataGridView1, "Multi Line Vertical")
```

Single Line Horizontal

```
Module1.do_dao_code_for_dataGridView(DataGridView1, "Single Line
Horizontal")
```

Single Line Vertical

```
Module1.do_dao_code_for_dataGridView(DataGridView1, "Single Line Vertical")
```

Dynamically binding to the Listview

Chapter Subtitle

```
Public Sub do_dao_code_for_ListView(ByVal lv As ListView, ByVal
Orientation As String)


    lv.Items.Clear()
    lv.Columns.Clear()


    Select Case Orientation


        Case "Multi Line Horizontal"

            For x As Integer = 0 To rs.Fields.Count - 1
```

```vbnet
        lv.Columns.Add(rs.Fields(x).Name)
    Next

    Dim li As ListViewItem = Nothing

    For y As Integer = 0 To rs.RecordCount - 1
        For x As Integer = 0 To rs.Fields.Count - 1
            If (x = 0) Then
                li = lv.Items.Add(rs.Fields(x).Value)
            Else
                li.SubItems.Add(rs.Fields(x).Value)
            End If
        Next
        rs.MoveNext()
    Next


Case "Multi Line Vertical"


    lv.Columns.Add("Property Name")
    For y As Integer = 0 To rs.RecordCount - 1
        lv.Columns.Add("Row" & y)
    Next

    Dim li As ListViewItem = Nothing

    For x As Integer = 0 To rs.Fields.Count - 1
        li = lv.Items.Add(rs.Fields(x).Name)
        rs.MoveFirst()
        For y As Integer = 0 To rs.RecordCount - 1
            li.SubItems.Add(rs.Fields(x).Value)
            rs.MoveNext()
        Next
    Next

Case "Single Line Horizontal"
```

```vbnet
        For x As Integer = 0 To rs.Fields.Count - 1
            lv.Columns.Add(rs.Fields(x).Name)
        Next

        Dim li As ListViewItem = Nothing

        For y As Integer = 0 To rs.RecordCount - 1
            For x As Integer = 0 To rs.Fields.Count - 1
                If (x = 0) Then
                    li = lv.Items.Add(rs.Fields(x).Value)
                Else
                    li.SubItems.Add(rs.Fields(x).Value)
                End If
            Next
            Exit For
        Next


    Case "Single Line Vertical"


        lv.Columns.Add("Property Name")
        lv.Columns.Add("Property Value")

        Dim li As ListViewItem = Nothing

        For x As Integer = 0 To rs.Fields.Count - 1
            li = lv.Items.Add(rs.Fields(x).Name)
            li.SubItems.Add(rs.Fields(x).Value)
        Next

    End Select

End Sub
```

Making the Listview work using DAO

This time, we use the following code:

```
Module1.Open_DAO_Recordset_Using_DBEngine("ODBC;Driver={Microsoft Access
Driver (*.mdb)};dbq=G:\nwind.mdb;", "Select * from [Products]")
```

```
Orientation:
```

```
Multi Line Horizontal
```

```
Module1.do_dao_code_for_ListView(ListView1, "Multi Line Horizontal")
```

```
Multi Line Vertical
```

```
Module1.do_dao_code_for_ListView(ListView1, "Multi Line Vertical")
```

```
Single Line Horizontal
```

```
Module1.do_dao_code_for_ListView(ListView1, "Single Line Horizontal")
```

```
Single Line Vertical
```

```
Module1.do_dao_code_for_ListView(ListView1, "Single Line Vertical")
```

Dynamically binding DAO to the MSFlexgrid

Chapter Subtitle

```
Public    Sub    do_dao_code_for_MSFlexGrid(ByVal    fg    As
AxMSFlexGridLib.AxMSFlexGrid, ByVal Orientation As String)


    fg.Clear()


    Select Case Orientation


        Case "Multi Line Horizontal"


            fg.Cols = rs.Fields.Count + 1
            fg.Rows = rs.RecordCount + 1
            For x As Integer = 0 To rs.Fields.Count - 1
                fg.set_TextMatrix(0, x + 1, rs.Fields(x).Name)
            Next

            rs.MoveFirst()
```

```
    For y As Integer = 0 To rs.RecordCount - 1
       For x As Integer = 0 To rs.Fields.Count - 1
          fg.set_TextMatrix(y + 1, x + 1, rs.Fields(x).Value)
       Next
       rs.MoveNext()
    Next


Case "Multi Line Vertical"

    fg.Rows = rs.Fields.Count + 1
    fg.Cols = rs.RecordCount + 1
    For x As Integer = 0 To rs.Fields.Count - 1
       fg.set_TextMatrix(x + 1, 0, rs.Fields(x).Name)
    Next

    For y As Integer = 0 To rs.RecordCount - 1
       For x As Integer = 0 To rs.Fields.Count - 1
          fg.set_TextMatrix(x + 1, y + 1, rs.Fields(x).Value)
       Next
    Next


Case "Single Line Horizontal"

    fg.Cols = rs.Fields.Count + 1
    fg.Rows = 2
    For x As Integer = 0 To rs.Fields.Count - 1
       fg.set_TextMatrix(0, x + 1, rs.Fields(x).Name)
    Next

    For y As Integer = 0 To rs.RecordCount - 1
       For x As Integer = 0 To rs.Fields.Count - 1
          fg.set_TextMatrix(y + 1, x + 1, rs.Fields(x).Value)
       Next
       Exit For
    Next
```

```
Case "Single Line Vertical"


    fg.Rows = rs.Fields.Count + 1
    fg.Cols = 2
    For x As Integer = 0 To rs.Fields.Count - 1
        fg.set_TextMatrix(x + 1, 0, rs.Fields(x).Name)
    Next

    For y As Integer = 0 To rs.RecordCount - 1
        For x As Integer = 0 To rs.Fields.Count - 1
            fg.set_TextMatrix(x + 1, y + 1, rs.Fields(x).Value)
        Next
        Exit For
    Next


End Select

End Sub
```

Making the MSFlexgrid work using DAO

These routines will get the job done:

```
Module1.Open_DAO_Recordset_Using_DBEngine("ODBC;Driver={Microsoft Access
Driver (*.mdb)};dbq=G:\nwind.mdb;", "Select * from [Products]")
```

Orientation:

Multi Line Horizontal

```
Module1.do_dao_code_for_MSFlexGrid(AxMSFlexGrid1
, "Multi Line Horizontal")
```

Multi Line Vertical

```
Module1.do_dao_code_for_MSFlexGrid(AxMSFlexGrid1
, "Multi Line Vertical")
```

Single Line Horizontal

```
Module1.do_dao_code_for_MSFlexGrid(AxMSFlexGrid1
, "Single Line Horizontal")
```

Single Line Vertical

```
Module1.do_dao_code_for_MSFlexGrid(AxMSFlexGrid1
, "Single Line Vertical")
```

Dynamically binding DAO to the Spreadsheet

Public Sub do_dao_code_for_Spreadsheet(ByVal sp1 As AxMicrosoft.Office.Interop.Owc11.AxSpreadsheet, ByVal Orientation As String)

```vb
    sp1.ActiveSheet.Cells.Clear()


    Select Case Orientation


        Case "Multi Line Horizontal"


            For x As Integer = 0 To rs.Fields.Count - 1
                sp1.ActiveSheet.Cells(1, x + 1) = rs.Fields(x).Name
            Next

            rs.MoveFirst()

            For y As Integer = 0 To rs.RecordCount - 1
                For x As Integer = 0 To rs.Fields.Count - 1
                    sp1.ActiveSheet.Cells(y + 1, x + 1) = rs.Fields(x).Value
```

```
            Next
            rs.MoveNext()
        Next



    Case "Multi Line Vertical"


        For x As Integer = 0 To rs.Fields.Count - 1
            sp1.ActiveSheet.Cells(x + 1, 1) = rs.Fields(x).Name
        Next

        For y As Integer = 0 To rs.RecordCount - 1
            rs.MoveFirst()
            For x As Integer = 0 To rs.Fields.Count - 1
                sp1.ActiveSheet.Cells(x + 1, y + 2) = rs.Fields(x).Value
            Next
            rs.MoveNext()
        Next



    Case "Single Line Horizontal"


        For x As Integer = 0 To rs.Fields.Count - 1
            sp1.ActiveSheet.Cells(1, x + 1) = rs.Fields(x).Name
        Next

    rs.MoveFirst()

        For y As Integer = 0 To rs.RecordCount - 1
            For x As Integer = 0 To rs.Fields.Count - 1
                sp1.ActiveSheet.Cells(y + 2, x + 1) = rs.Fields(x).Value
            Next
            Exit For
        Next



    Case "Single Line Vertical"
```

```vb
    For x As Integer = 0 To rs.Fields.Count - 1
        sp1.ActiveSheet.Cells(x + 1, 1) = rs.Fields(x).Name
    Next

    rs.MoveFirst()

    For y As Integer = 0 To rs.RecordCount - 1
        For x As Integer = 0 To rs.Fields.Count - 1
            sp1.ActiveSheet.Cells(x + 1, y + 2) = rs.Fields(x).Value
        Next
        Exit For
    Next


    End Select

End Sub
```

Making the Spreadsheet work using DAO

Routines for the Spreadsheet will get the job done:

```
Module1.Open_DAO_Recordset_Using_DBEngine("ODBC;Driver={Microsoft Access Driver (*.mdb)};dbq=G:\nwind.mdb;", "Select * from [Products]")
```

Orientation:

Multi Line Horizontal

```
Module1.do_dao_code_for_Spreadsheet(AxSpreadsheet1, "Multi Line Horizontal")
```

Multi Line Vertical

```
Module1.do_dao_code_for_Spreadsheet(AxSpreadsheet1, "Multi Line Vertical")
```

Single Line Horizontal

```
Module1.do_dao_code_for_Spreadsheet(AxSpreadsheet1, "Single Line Horizontal")
```

Single Line Vertical

```
Module1.do_dao_code_for_Spreadsheet(AxSpreadsheet1, "Single Line Vertical")
```

Working with the DataGridView using A DataSet

```
Public Sub do_DataSet_code_for_dataGridView(ByVal DG As
DataGridView, ByVal Orientation As String)


        DG.Rows.Clear()
        DG.Columns.Clear()


        Select Case Orientation


            Case "Multi Line Horizontal"

                For x As Integer = 0 To
ds.Tables(0).Columns.Count - 1

DG.Columns.Add(ds.Tables(0).Columns(x).Caption,
ds.Tables(0).Columns(x).Caption)
                Next


                For y As Integer = 0 To ds.Tables(0).Rows.Count -
1
                    DG.Rows.Add()
                    For x As Integer = 0 To
ds.Tables(0).Columns.Count - 1
                        DG.Rows(y).Cells(x).Value =
ds.Tables(0).Rows(y).Item(ds.Tables(0).Columns(x).Caption)
                    Next
```

```vbnet
                rs.MoveNext()
          Next


      Case "Multi Line Vertical"


          DG.Columns.Add("Property Name", "Property Name")
          For y As Integer = 0 To ds.Tables(0).Rows.Count -
1
              DG.Columns.Add("Row" & y, "Row" & y)
          Next

          For x As Integer = 0 To
ds.Tables(0).Columns.Count - 1
              DG.Rows.Add()
              DG.Rows(x).Cells(0).Value =
ds.Tables(0).Columns(x).Caption
              For y As Integer = 0 To
ds.Tables(0).Rows.Count - 1
                  DG.Rows(x).Cells(y + 1).Value =
ds.Tables(0).Rows(y).Item(ds.Tables(0).Columns(x).Caption)
              Next
          Next

      Case "Single Line Horizontal"


          For x As Integer = 0 To
ds.Tables(0).Columns.Count - 1

DG.Columns.Add(ds.Tables(0).Columns(x).Caption,
ds.Tables(0).Columns(x).Caption)
          Next

          For y As Integer = 0 To ds.Tables(0).Rows.Count -
1
              DG.Rows.Add()
              For x As Integer = 0 To
ds.Tables(0).Columns.Count - 1
                  DG.Rows(y).Cells(x).Value =
ds.Tables(0).Rows(y).Item(ds.Tables(0).Columns(x).Caption)
              Next
              Exit For
          Next
```

```vbnet
            Case "Single Line Vertical"


                DG.Columns.Add("Property Name", "Property Name")
                DG.Columns.Add("Property Value", "Property
Value")

                For x As Integer = 0 To
ds.Tables(0).Columns.Count - 1
                    DG.Rows.Add()
                    DG.Rows(x).Cells(0).Value =
ds.Tables(0).Columns(x).Caption
                    DG.Rows(x).Cells(1).Value =
ds.Tables(0).Rows(0).Item(ds.Tables(0).Columns(x).Caption)
                Next

        End Select

    End Sub
```

Making the DataGridView work using a DataSet

To make this code work, we piece together three routines:

Module1.Open_DAO_Recordset_Using_DBEngine("ODBC;Driver={Microsoft Access Driver (*.mdb)};dbq=G:\nwind.mdb;", "Select * from [Products]")
Module1.Create_DataSet_using_DAO_Recordset_Using_DBEngine("Multi Line Horizontal")

Now, depending on what view we want to create:

Orientation:

Multi Line Horizontal

Module1.do_DataSet_code_for_DataGridView(DataGridView1, "Multi Line Horizontal")

Multi Line Vertical

Module1.do_DataSet_code_for_ DataGridView(DataGridView1, "Multi Line Vertical")

Single Line Horizontal

Module1.do_DataSet_code_for_ DataGridView(DataGridView1, "Single Line Horizontal")

Single Line Vertical

Working with the DataGridView using a DataTable

```
Public Sub do_DataTable_code_for_dataGridView(ByVal DG As
DataGridView, ByVal Orientation As String)


        DG.Rows.Clear()
        DG.Columns.Clear()


        Select Case Orientation


            Case "Multi Line Horizontal"

                For x As Integer = 0 To dt.Columns.Count - 1
                    DG.Columns.Add(dt.Columns(x).Caption,
dt.Columns(x).Caption)
                Next

                For y As Integer = 0 To dt.Rows.Count - 1
                    DG.Rows.Add()
                    For x As Integer = 0 To dt.Columns.Count - 1
```

```vb
                                DG.Rows(y).Cells(x).Value =
dt.Rows(y).Item(dt.Columns(x).Caption)
                        Next
                        rs.MoveNext()
                Next


        Case "Multi Line Vertical"


                DG.Columns.Add("Property Name", "Property Name")
                For y As Integer = 0 To dt.Rows.Count - 1
                    DG.Columns.Add("Row" & y, "Row" & y)
                Next

                For x As Integer = 0 To dt.Columns.Count - 1
                    DG.Rows.Add()
                    DG.Rows(x).Cells(0).Value =
dt.Columns(x).Caption
                        For y As Integer = 0 To dt.Rows.Count - 1
                            DG.Rows(x).Cells(y + 1).Value =
dt.Rows(y).Item(dt.Columns(x).Caption)
                        Next
                Next

        Case "Single Line Horizontal"


                For x As Integer = 0 To dt.Columns.Count - 1
                    DG.Columns.Add(dt.Columns(x).Caption,
dt.Columns(x).Caption)
                Next

                For y As Integer = 0 To dt.Rows.Count - 1
                    DG.Rows.Add()
                    For x As Integer = 0 To dt.Columns.Count - 1
                        DG.Rows(y).Cells(x).Value =
dt.Rows(y).Item(dt.Columns(x).Caption)
                    Next
                    Exit For
                Next


        Case "Single Line Vertical"
```

```vbnet
                DG.Columns.Add("Property Name", "Property Name")
                DG.Columns.Add("Property Value", "Property
Value")

                For x As Integer = 0 To dt.Columns.Count - 1
                    DG.Rows.Add()
                    DG.Rows(x).Cells(0).Value =
dt.Columns(x).Caption
                    DG.Rows(x).Cells(1).Value =
dt.Rows(0).Item(dt.Columns(x).Caption)
                Next

        End Select

    End Sub
```

Making the DataGridView work using a DataTable

To make this code work, we piece together three routines:

Module1.Open_DAO_Recordset_Using_DBEngine("ODBC;Driver={Microsoft Access Driver (*.mdb)};dbq=G:\nwind.mdb;", "Select * from [Products]")
Module1.Create_DataTable_using_DAO_Recordset_Using_DBEngine("Multi Line Horizontal")

Now, depending on what view we want to create:

Orientation:

Multi Line Horizontal

Module1.do_DataTable_code_for_DataGridView(DataGridView1, "Multi Line Horizontal")

Multi Line Vertical

Module1.do_DataTable_code_for_ DataGridView(DataGridView1, "Multi Line Vertical")

Single Line Horizontal

Module1.do_DataTable_code_for_ DataGridView(DataGridView1, "Single Line Horizontal")

Single Line Vertical

Working with the DataGridView using A DataView

```vb
Public Sub do_DataView_code_for_dataGridView(ByVal DG As
DataGridView, ByVal Orientation As String)


    DG.Rows.Clear()
    DG.Columns.Clear()


    Select Case Orientation


        Case "Multi Line Horizontal"

            For x As Integer = 0 To dv.Table.Columns.Count -
1
                DG.Columns.Add(dv.Table.Columns(x).Caption,
dv.Table.Columns(x).Caption)
            Next

            For y As Integer = 0 To dv.Table.Rows.Count - 1
```

```vbnet
                        DG.Rows.Add()
                        For x As Integer = 0 To
dv.Table.Columns.Count - 1
                            DG.Rows(y).Cells(x).Value =
dv.Table.Rows(y).Item(dv.Table.Columns(x).Caption)
                        Next
                        rs.MoveNext()
                    Next


            Case "Multi Line Vertical"


                DG.Columns.Add("Property Name", "Property Name")
                For y As Integer = 0 To dv.Table.Rows.Count - 1
                    DG.Columns.Add("Row" & y, "Row" & y)
                Next

                For x As Integer = 0 To dv.Table.Columns.Count -
1
                    DG.Rows.Add()
                    DG.Rows(x).Cells(0).Value =
dv.Table.Columns(x).Caption
                    For y As Integer = 0 To dv.Table.Rows.Count -
1
                        DG.Rows(x).Cells(y + 1).Value =
dv.Table.Rows(y).Item(dv.Table.Columns(x).Caption)
                    Next
                Next

            Case "Single Line Horizontal"


                For x As Integer = 0 To dv.Table.Columns.Count -
1
                    DG.Columns.Add(dv.Table.Columns(x).Caption,
dv.Table.Columns(x).Caption)
                Next

                For y As Integer = 0 To dv.Table.Rows.Count - 1
                    DG.Rows.Add()
                    For x As Integer = 0 To
dv.Table.Columns.Count - 1
                        DG.Rows(y).Cells(x).Value =
dv.Table.Rows(y).Item(dv.Table.Columns(x).Caption)
```

```
                    Next
                    Exit For
            Next


        Case "Single Line Vertical"


            DG.Columns.Add("Property Name", "Property Name")
            DG.Columns.Add("Property Value", "Property
Value")

            For x As Integer = 0 To dv.Table.Columns.Count -
1
                DG.Rows.Add()
                DG.Rows(x).Cells(0).Value =
dv.Table.Columns(x).Caption
                DG.Rows(x).Cells(1).Value =
dv.Table.Rows(0).Item(dv.Table.Columns(x).Caption)
            Next

        End Select

    End Sub
```

Making the DataGridView work using a DataView

To make this code work, we piece together three routines:

Module1.Open_DAO_Recordset_Using_DBEngine("ODBC;Driver={Microsoft Access Driver (*.mdb)};dbq=G:\nwind.mdb;", "Select * from [Products]")
Module1.Create_DataView_using_DAO_Recordset_Using_DBEngine("Multi Line Horizontal")

Now, depending on what view we want to create:

Orientation:

Multi Line Horizontal

Module1.do_DataView_code_for_DataGridView(DataGridView1, "Multi Line Horizontal")

Multi Line Vertical

Module1.do_DataView_code_for_ DataGridView(DataGridView1, "Multi Line Vertical")

Single Line Horizontal

Module1.do_DataView_code_for_ DataGridView(DataGridView1, "Single Line Horizontal")

Single Line Vertical

Module1.do_DataView_code_for_ DataGridView(DataGridView1, "Single Line Vertical")

Working with the Listview using a DataSet

Chapter Subtitle

```vb
Public Sub do_DataSet_code_for_ListView(ByVal lv As ListView, ByVal
Orientation As String)


    lv.Items.Clear()
    lv.Columns.Clear()


    Select Case Orientation


        Case "Multi Line Horizontal"

            For x As Integer = 0 To ds.Tables(0).Columns.Count - 1
                lv.Columns.Add(ds.Tables(0).Columns(x).Caption)
            Next

            Dim li As ListViewItem = Nothing

            For y As Integer = 0 To ds.Tables(0).Rows.Count - 1
```

```vb
                    For x As Integer = 0 To ds.Tables(0).Columns.Count - 1
                        If (x = 0) Then
                            li                                                              =
lv.Items.Add(ds.Tables(0).Rows(y).Item(ds.Tables(0).Columns(x)))
                        Else

li.SubItems.Add(ds.Tables(0).Rows(y).Item(ds.Tables(0).Columns(x)))
                        End If
                    Next
                Next


            Case "Multi Line Vertical"


                lv.Columns.Add("Property Name")
                For y As Integer = 0 To ds.Tables(0).Rows.Count - 1
                    lv.Columns.Add("Row" & y)
                Next

                Dim li As ListViewItem = Nothing

                For x As Integer = 0 To ds.Tables(0).Columns.Count - 1
                    li = lv.Items.Add(ds.Tables(0).Columns(x).Caption)
                    For y As Integer = 0 To ds.Tables(0).Rows.Count - 1

li.SubItems.Add(ds.Tables(0).Rows(y).Item(ds.Tables(0).Columns(x).Caption))
                    Next
                Next

            Case "Single Line Horizontal"


                For x As Integer = 0 To ds.Tables(0).Columns.Count - 1
                    lv.Columns.Add(ds.Tables(0).Columns(x).Caption)
                Next

                Dim li As ListViewItem = Nothing

                For y As Integer = 0 To ds.Tables(0).Rows.Count - 1
```

```vb
                For x As Integer = 0 To ds.Tables(0).Columns.Count - 1
                    If (x = 0) Then
                        li                                                                =
lv.Items.Add(ds.Tables(0).Rows(y).Item(ds.Tables(0).Columns(x).Caption))
                    Else

li.SubItems.Add(ds.Tables(0).Rows(y).Item(ds.Tables(0).Columns(x).Caption))
                    End If
                Next
                Exit For
            Next


        Case "Single Line Vertical"


            lv.Columns.Add("Property Name")
            lv.Columns.Add("Property Value")

            Dim li As ListViewItem = Nothing

            For x As Integer = 0 To ds.Tables(0).Columns.Count - 1
                li = lv.Items.Add(ds.Tables(0).Columns(x).Caption)

li.SubItems.Add(ds.Tables(0).Rows(0).Item(ds.Tables(0).Columns(x)))
            Next

    End Select

    End Sub
```

Making the Listview using a DataSet work

To make this code work, we piece together three routines:

Module1.Open_DAO_Recordset_Using_DBEngine("ODBC;Driver={Microsoft Access Driver (*.mdb)};dbq=G:\nwind.mdb;", "Select * from [Products]")
Module1.Create_DataSet_using_DAO_Recordset_Using_DBEngine("Multi Line Horizontal")

Now, depending on what view we want to create:

Orientation:

Multi Line Horizontal

Module1.do_DataSet_code_for_ListView(ListView1, "Multi Line Horizontal")

Multi Line Vertical

Module1.do_DataSet_code_for_ListView(ListView1, "Multi Line Vertical")

Single Line Horizontal

Module1.do_DataSet_code_for_ListView(ListView1, "Single Line Horizontal")

Single Line Vertical

Module1.do_DataSet_code_for_ListView(ListView1, "Single Line Vertical")

Working with the Listview using a DataTable

```vb
Public Sub do_DataTable_code_for_ListView(ByVal lv As ListView, ByVal
Orientation As String)


    lv.Items.Clear()
    lv.Columns.Clear()


    Select Case Orientation


        Case "Multi Line Horizontal"

            For x As Integer = 0 To dt.Columns.Count - 1
                lv.Columns.Add(dt.Columns(x).Caption)
            Next

            Dim li As ListViewItem = Nothing

            For y As Integer = 0 To dt.Rows.Count - 1
                For x As Integer = 0 To dt.Columns.Count - 1
                    If (x = 0) Then
                        li = lv.Items.Add(dt.Rows(y).Item(dt.Columns(x)))
                    Else
```

```vbnet
                    li.SubItems.Add(dt.Rows(y).Item(dt.Columns(x)))
                End If
            Next
        Next


    Case "Multi Line Vertical"


        lv.Columns.Add("Property Name")
        For y As Integer = 0 To dt.Rows.Count - 1
            lv.Columns.Add("Row" & y)
        Next

        Dim li As ListViewItem = Nothing

        For x As Integer = 0 To dt.Columns.Count - 1
            li = lv.Items.Add(dt.Columns(x).Caption)
            For y As Integer = 0 To dt.Rows.Count - 1
                li.SubItems.Add(dt.Rows(y).Item(dt.Columns(x).Caption))
            Next
        Next

    Case "Single Line Horizontal"


        For x As Integer = 0 To dt.Columns.Count - 1
            lv.Columns.Add(dt.Columns(x).Caption)
        Next

        Dim li As ListViewItem = Nothing

        For y As Integer = 0 To dt.Rows.Count - 1
            For x As Integer = 0 To dt.Columns.Count - 1
                If (x = 0) Then
                    li = lv.Items.Add(dt.Rows(y).Item(dt.Columns(x).Caption))
                Else
                    li.SubItems.Add(dt.Rows(y).Item(dt.Columns(x).Caption))
                End If
            Next
```

```vbnet
                Exit For
        Next


    Case "Single Line Vertical"


        lv.Columns.Add("Property Name")
        lv.Columns.Add("Property Value")

        Dim li As ListViewItem = Nothing

        For x As Integer = 0 To dt.Columns.Count - 1
            li = lv.Items.Add(dt.Columns(x).Caption)
            li.SubItems.Add(dt.Rows(0).Item(dt.Columns(x)))
        Next

    End Select

End Sub
```

Making the Listview using a DataTable work

Same routine as the DataSet. Just some name changes:

Module1.Open_DAO_Recordset_Using_DBEngine("ODBC;Driver={Microsoft Access Driver (*.mdb)};dbq=G:\nwind.mdb;", "Select * from [Products]")
Module1.Create_DataTable_using_DAO_Recordset_Using_DBEngine("Multi Line Horizontal")

Now, depending on what view we want to create:

Orientation:

Multi Line Horizontal

Module1.do_DataTable_code_for_ListView(ListView1, "Multi Line Horizontal")

Multi Line Vertical

Module1.do_DataTable_code_for_ListView(ListView1, "Multi Line Vertical")

Single Line Horizontal

Module1.do_DataTable_code_for_ListView(ListView1, "Single Line Horizontal")

Single Line Vertical

Module1.do_DataTable_code_for_ListView(ListView1, "Single Line Vertical")

Working with the Listview using a DataView

```vb
Public Sub do_DataView_code_for_ListView(ByVal lv As ListView, ByVal
Orientation As String)


    lv.Items.Clear()
    lv.Columns.Clear()


    Select Case Orientation


        Case "Multi Line Horizontal"

            For x As Integer = 0 To dv.Table.Columns.Count - 1
                lv.Columns.Add(dv.Table.Columns(x).Caption)
            Next

            Dim li As ListViewItem = Nothing

            For y As Integer = 0 To dv.Table.Rows.Count - 1
                For x As Integer = 0 To dv.Table.Columns.Count - 1
                    If (x = 0) Then
                        li = lv.Items.Add(dv.Table.Rows(y).Item(dv.Table.Columns(x)))
                    Else
```

```vbnet
                li.SubItems.Add(dv.Table.Rows(y).Item(dv.Table.Columns(x)))
            End If
        Next
    Next


Case "Multi Line Vertical"


    lv.Columns.Add("Property Name")
    For y As Integer = 0 To dv.Table.Rows.Count - 1
        lv.Columns.Add("Row" & y)
    Next

    Dim li As ListViewItem = Nothing

    For x As Integer = 0 To dv.Table.Columns.Count - 1
        li = lv.Items.Add(dv.Table.Columns(x).Caption)
        For y As Integer = 0 To dv.Table.Rows.Count - 1

li.SubItems.Add(dv.Table.Rows(y).Item(dv.Table.Columns(x).Caption))
        Next
    Next

Case "Single Line Horizontal"


    For x As Integer = 0 To dv.Table.Columns.Count - 1
        lv.Columns.Add(dv.Table.Columns(x).Caption)
    Next

    Dim li As ListViewItem = Nothing

    For y As Integer = 0 To dv.Table.Rows.Count - 1
        For x As Integer = 0 To dv.Table.Columns.Count - 1
            If (x = 0) Then
                li                                                      =
lv.Items.Add(dv.Table.Rows(y).Item(dv.Table.Columns(x).Caption))
            Else
```

```vbnet
li.SubItems.Add(dv.Table.Rows(y).Item(dv.Table.Columns(x).Caption))
                End If
            Next
            Exit For
        Next


    Case "Single Line Vertical"


        lv.Columns.Add("Property Name")
        lv.Columns.Add("Property Value")

        Dim li As ListViewItem = Nothing

        For x As Integer = 0 To dv.Table.Columns.Count - 1
            li = lv.Items.Add(dv.Table.Columns(x).Caption)
            li.SubItems.Add(dv.Table.Rows(0).Item(dv.Table.Columns(x)))
        Next

    End Select

End Sub
```

Making the Listview using a DataView work

Here's the routine:

Module1.Open_DAO_Recordset_Using_DBEngine("ODBC;Driver={Microsoft Access Driver (*.mdb)};dbq=G:\nwind.mdb;", "Select * from [Products]")
Module1.Create_DataView_using_DAO_Recordset_Using_DBEngine("Multi Line Horizontal")

Now, depending on what view we want to create:

Orientation:

Multi Line Horizontal

Module1.do_DataView_code_for_ListView(ListView1, "Multi Line Horizontal")

Multi Line Vertical

Module1.do_DataView_code_for_ListView(ListView1, "Multi Line Vertical")

Single Line Horizontal

Module1.do_DataView_code_for_ListView(ListView1, "Single Line Horizontal")

Single Line Vertical

Module1.do_DataView_code_for_ListView(ListView1, "Single Line Vertical")

Working with the MSFlexgrid using a Dataset

Chapter Subtitle

```
Public     Sub     do_DataSet_code_for_MSFlexGrid(ByVal     fg     As
AxMSFlexGridLib.AxMSFlexGrid, ByVal Orientation As String)


    fg.Clear()


    Select Case Orientation


        Case "Multi Line Horizontal"


            fg.Cols = ds.Tables(0).Columns.Count + 1
            fg.Rows = ds.Tables(0).Rows.Count + 1
            For x As Integer = 0 To ds.Tables(0).Columns.Count - 1
                fg.set_TextMatrix(0, x + 1, ds.Tables(0).Columns(x).Caption)
            Next
```

```
                For y As Integer = 0 To ds.Tables(0).Rows.Count - 1
                    For x As Integer = 0 To ds.Tables(0).Columns.Count - 1
                        fg.set_TextMatrix(y          +          1,          x          +          1,
ds.Tables(0).Rows(y).Item(ds.Tables(0).Columns(x).Caption))
                    Next
                Next


        Case "Multi Line Vertical"

                fg.Rows = ds.Tables(0).Columns.Count + 1
                fg.Cols = ds.Tables(0).Rows.Count + 1
                For x As Integer = 0 To ds.Tables(0).Columns.Count - 1
                    fg.set_TextMatrix(x + 1, 0, ds.Tables(0).Columns(x).Caption)
                Next

                For y As Integer = 0 To ds.Tables(0).Rows.Count - 1
                    For x As Integer = 0 To ds.Tables(0).Columns.Count - 1
                        fg.set_TextMatrix(x          +          1,          y          +          1,
ds.Tables(0).Rows(y).Item(ds.Tables(0).Columns(x).Caption))
                    Next
                Next


        Case "Single Line Horizontal"


                fg.Cols = ds.Tables(0).Columns.Count + 1
                fg.Rows = 2
                For x As Integer = 0 To ds.Tables(0).Columns.Count - 1
                    fg.set_TextMatrix(0, x + 1, ds.Tables(0).Columns(x).Caption)
                Next

                For y As Integer = 0 To ds.Tables(0).Rows.Count - 1
                    For x As Integer = 0 To ds.Tables(0).Columns.Count - 1
                        fg.set_TextMatrix(y          +          1,          x          +          1,
ds.Tables(0).Rows(y).Item(ds.Tables(0).Columns(x).Caption))
                    Next
                    Exit For
                Next
```

```
Case "Single Line Vertical"

    fg.Rows = ds.Tables(0).Columns.Count + 1
    fg.Cols = 2
    For x As Integer = 0 To ds.Tables(0).Columns.Count - 1
        fg.set_TextMatrix(x + 1, 0, ds.Tables(0).Columns(x).Caption)
    Next

    For y As Integer = 0 To ds.Tables(0).Rows.Count - 1
        For x As Integer = 0 To ds.Tables(0).Columns.Count - 1
            fg.set_TextMatrix(x + 1, y + 1, ds.Tables(0).Rows(y).Item(ds.Tables(0).Columns(x).Caption))
        Next
        Exit For
    Next



End Select

End Sub
```

Making the MSFlexgrid using a DataSet work

Module1.Open_DAO_Recordset_Using_DBEngine("ODBC;Driver={Microsoft Access Driver (*.mdb)};dbq=G:\nwind.mdb;", "Select * from [Products]")
Module1.Create_DataSet_using_DAO_Recordset_Using_DBEngine("Multi Line Horizontal")

Now, depending on what view we want to create:

Orientation:

Multi Line Horizontal

Module1.do_DataSet_code_for_MSFlexGrid (AxMSFlexGrid1
, "Multi Line Horizontal")

Multi Line Vertical

Module1.do_DataSet_code_for_MSFlexGrid(AxMSFlexGrid1
, "Multi Line Vertical")

Single Line Horizontal

Module1.do_DataSet_code_for_MSFlexGrid(AxMSFlexGrid1
, "Single Line Horizontal")

Single Line Vertical

Module1.do_DataSet_code_for_MSFlexGrid(AxMSFlexGrid1
, "Single Line Vertical")

Working with the MSFlexgrid using a DataTable

Chapter Subtitle

```vb
Public    Sub    do_DataTable_code_for_MSFlexGrid(ByVal    fg    As
AxMSFlexGridLib.AxMSFlexGrid, ByVal Orientation As String)


    fg.Clear()


    Select Case Orientation


        Case "Multi Line Horizontal"


            fg.Cols = dt.Columns.Count + 1
            fg.Rows = dt.Rows.Count + 1
            For x As Integer = 0 To dt.Columns.Count - 1
                fg.set_TextMatrix(0, x + 1, dt.Columns(x).Caption)
            Next

            For y As Integer = 0 To dt.Rows.Count - 1
                For x As Integer = 0 To dt.Columns.Count - 1
```

```vb
                    fg.set_TextMatrix(y          +          1,          x          +          1,
dt.Rows(y).Item(dt.Columns(x).Caption))
                Next
            Next


        Case "Multi Line Vertical"

            fg.Rows = dt.Columns.Count + 1
            fg.Cols = dt.Rows.Count + 1
            For x As Integer = 0 To dt.Columns.Count - 1
                fg.set_TextMatrix(x + 1, 0, dt.Columns(x).Caption)
            Next

            For y As Integer = 0 To dt.Rows.Count - 1
                For x As Integer = 0 To dt.Columns.Count - 1
                    fg.set_TextMatrix(x          +          1,          y          +          1,
dt.Rows(y).Item(dt.Columns(x).Caption))
                Next
            Next


        Case "Single Line Horizontal"


            fg.Cols = dt.Columns.Count + 1
            fg.Rows = 2
            For x As Integer = 0 To dt.Columns.Count - 1
                fg.set_TextMatrix(0, x + 1, dt.Columns(x).Caption)
            Next

            For y As Integer = 0 To dt.Rows.Count - 1
                For x As Integer = 0 To dt.Columns.Count - 1
                    fg.set_TextMatrix(y          +          1,          x          +          1,
dt.Rows(y).Item(dt.Columns(x).Caption))
                Next
                Exit For
            Next
```

```vbnet
Case "Single Line Vertical"

    fg.Rows = dt.Columns.Count + 1
    fg.Cols = 2
    For x As Integer = 0 To dt.Columns.Count - 1
        fg.set_TextMatrix(x + 1, 0, dt.Columns(x).Caption)
    Next

    For y As Integer = 0 To dt.Rows.Count - 1
        For x As Integer = 0 To dt.Columns.Count - 1
            fg.set_TextMatrix(x       +       1,       y       +       1,
dt.Rows(y).Item(dt.Columns(x).Caption))
        Next
        Exit For
    Next



End Select

End Sub
```

Making the MSFlexgrid using a DataTable work

Routines to make the magic happen:

Module1.Open_DAO_Recordset_Using_DBEngine("ODBC;Driver={Microsoft Access Driver (*.mdb)};dbq=G:\nwind.mdb;", "Select * from [Products]")
Module1.Create_DataTable_using_DAO_Recordset_Using_DBEngine("Multi Line Horizontal")

Now, depending on what view we want to create:

Orientation:

Multi Line Horizontal

Module1.do_DataTable_code_for_MSFlexGrid (AxMSFlexGrid1 , "Multi Line Horizontal")

Multi Line Vertical

Module1.do_DataTable_code_for_MSFlexGrid(AxMSFlexGrid1 , "Multi Line Vertical")

Single Line Horizontal

Module1.do_DataTable_code_for_MSFlexGrid(AxMSFlexGrid1 , "Single Line Horizontal")

Single Line Vertical

Module1.do_DataTable_code_for_MSFlexGrid(AxMSFlexGrid1

, "Single Line Vertical")

Working with the MSFlexGrid using a DataView
Chapter Subtitle

```
Public      Sub      do_DataView_code_for_MSFlexGrid(ByVal      fg      As
AxMSFlexGridLib.AxMSFlexGrid, ByVal Orientation As String)


    fg.Clear()


    Select Case Orientation


        Case "Multi Line Horizontal"
```

```
fg.Cols = dv.Table.Columns.Count + 1
fg.Rows = dv.Table.Rows.Count + 1
For x As Integer = 0 To dv.Table.Columns.Count - 1
    fg.set_TextMatrix(0, x + 1, dv.Table.Columns(x).Caption)
Next

For y As Integer = 0 To dv.Table.Rows.Count - 1
    For x As Integer = 0 To dv.Table.Columns.Count - 1
        fg.set_TextMatrix(y     +     1,     x     +     1,
dv.Table.Rows(y).Item(dv.Table.Columns(x).Caption))
    Next
Next


Case "Multi Line Vertical"

fg.Rows = dv.Table.Columns.Count + 1
fg.Cols = dv.Table.Rows.Count + 1
For x As Integer = 0 To dv.Table.Columns.Count - 1
    fg.set_TextMatrix(x + 1, 0, dv.Table.Columns(x).Caption)
Next

For y As Integer = 0 To dv.Table.Rows.Count - 1
    For x As Integer = 0 To dv.Table.Columns.Count - 1
        fg.set_TextMatrix(x     +     1,     y     +     1,
dv.Table.Rows(y).Item(dv.Table.Columns(x).Caption))
    Next
Next


Case "Single Line Horizontal"

fg.Cols = dv.Table.Columns.Count + 1
fg.Rows = 2
For x As Integer = 0 To dv.Table.Columns.Count - 1
    fg.set_TextMatrix(0, x + 1, dv.Table.Columns(x).Caption)
Next
```

```vb
        For y As Integer = 0 To dv.Table.Rows.Count - 1
            For x As Integer = 0 To dv.Table.Columns.Count - 1
                fg.set_TextMatrix(y        +        1,        x        +        1,
dv.Table.Rows(y).Item(dv.Table.Columns(x).Caption))
            Next
            Exit For
        Next


    Case "Single Line Vertical"

        fg.Rows = dv.Table.Columns.Count + 1
        fg.Cols = 2
        For x As Integer = 0 To dv.Table.Columns.Count - 1
            fg.set_TextMatrix(x + 1, 0, dv.Table.Columns(x).Caption)
        Next

        For y As Integer = 0 To dv.Table.Rows.Count - 1
            For x As Integer = 0 To dv.Table.Columns.Count - 1
                fg.set_TextMatrix(x        +        1,        y        +        1,
dv.Table.Rows(y).Item(dv.Table.Columns(x).Caption))
            Next
            Exit For
        Next



    End Select

    End Sub
```

Making the MSFlexgrid using a DataView work

The Routines:

Module1.Open_DAO_Recordset_Using_DBEngine("ODBC;Driver={Microsoft Access Driver (*.mdb)};dbq=G:\nwind.mdb;", "Select * from [Products]")
Module1.Create_DataView_using_DAO_Recordset_Using_DBEngine("Multi Line Horizontal")

Now, depending on what view we want to create:

Orientation:

Multi Line Horizontal

Module1.do_DataView_code_for_MSFlexGrid (AxMSFlexGrid1
, "Multi Line Horizontal")

Multi Line Vertical

Module1.do_DataView_code_for_MSFlexGrid(AxMSFlexGrid1
, "Multi Line Vertical")

Single Line Horizontal

Module1.do_DataView_code_for_MSFlexGrid(AxMSFlexGrid1
, "Single Line Horizontal")

Single Line Vertical

Module1.do_DataView_code_for_MSFlexGrid(AxMSFlexGrid1
, "Single Line Vertical")

Working with the Spreadsheet using a DataSet
Chapter Subtitle

```
Public    Sub    do_DataSet_code_for_Spreadsheet(ByVal    sp1    As
AxMicrosoft.Office.Interop.Owc11.AxSpreadsheet, ByVal Orientation As String)


    sp1.ActiveSheet.Cells.Clear()
```

```
Select Case Orientation


    Case "Multi Line Horizontal"


        For x As Integer = 0 To ds.Tables(0).Columns.Count - 1
            sp1.ActiveSheet.Cells(1, x + 1) = ds.Tables(0).Columns(x).Caption
        Next

        For y As Integer = 0 To ds.Tables(0).Rows.Count - 1
            For x As Integer = 0 To ds.Tables(0).Columns.Count - 1
                sp1.ActiveSheet.Cells(y     +     2,     x     +     1)     =
ds.Tables(0).Rows(y).Item(ds.Tables(0).Columns(x).Caption)
            Next
        Next


    Case "Multi Line Vertical"

        For x As Integer = 0 To ds.Tables(0).Columns.Count - 1
            sp1.ActiveSheet.Cells(x + 1, 1) = ds.Tables(0).Columns(x).Caption
        Next

        For y As Integer = 0 To ds.Tables(0).Rows.Count - 1
            For x As Integer = 0 To ds.Tables(0).Columns.Count - 1
                sp1.ActiveSheet.Cells(x     +     1,     y     +     2)     =
ds.Tables(0).Rows(y).Item(ds.Tables(0).Columns(x).Caption)
            Next
        Next


    Case "Single Line Horizontal"


        For x As Integer = 0 To ds.Tables(0).Columns.Count - 1
            sp1.ActiveSheet.Cells(1, x + 1) = ds.Tables(0).Columns(x).Caption
        Next

        For y As Integer = 0 To ds.Tables(0).Rows.Count - 1
```

```vbnet
            For x As Integer = 0 To ds.Tables(0).Columns.Count - 1
                sp1.ActiveSheet.Cells(y      +      2,      x      +      1)      =
ds.Tables(0).Rows(y).Item(ds.Tables(0).Columns(x).Caption)
            Next
            Exit For
        Next


    Case "Single Line Vertical"


        For x As Integer = 0 To ds.Tables(0).Columns.Count - 1
            sp1.ActiveSheet.Cells(x + 1, 1) = ds.Tables(0).Columns(x).Caption
        Next

        For y As Integer = 0 To ds.Tables(0).Rows.Count - 1
            For x As Integer = 0 To ds.Tables(0).Columns.Count - 1
                sp1.ActiveSheet.Cells(x      +      1,      y      +      2)      =
ds.Tables(0).Rows(y).Item(ds.Tables(0).Columns(x).Caption)
            Next
            Exit For
        Next


    End Select

    End Sub
```

Making the Spreadsheet using a DataSet work

This will get it done:

Module1.Open_DAO_Recordset_Using_DBEngine("ODBC;Driver={Microsoft Access Driver (*.mdb)};dbq=G:\nwind.mdb;", "Select * from [Products]")
Module1.Create_DataSet_using_DAO_Recordset_Using_DBEngine("Multi Line Horizontal")

Now, depending on what view we want to create:

Orientation:

Multi Line Horizontal

Module1.do_DataSet_code_for_Spreadsheet (AxSpreadsheet1

, "Multi Line Horizontal")

Multi Line Vertical

Module1.do_DataSet_code_for_Spreadsheet(AxSpreadsheet1

, "Multi Line Vertical")

Single Line Horizontal

Module1.do_DataSet_code_for_Spreadsheet(AxSpreadsheet1
, "Single Line Horizontal")

Single Line Vertical

Module1.do_DataSet_code_for_Spreadsheet(AxSpreadsheet1
, "Single Line Vertical")

Working with the Spreadsheet using a DataTable

Chapter Subtitle

```
Public    Sub    do_DataTable_code_for_Spreadsheet(ByVal    sp1    As
AxMicrosoft.Office.Interop.Owc11.AxSpreadsheet, ByVal Orientation As String)


    sp1.ActiveSheet.Cells.Clear()


    Select Case Orientation


        Case "Multi Line Horizontal"


            For x As Integer = 0 To dt.Columns.Count - 1
                sp1.ActiveSheet.Cells(1, x + 1) = dt.Columns(x).Caption
            Next

            For y As Integer = 0 To dt.Rows.Count - 1
                For x As Integer = 0 To dt.Columns.Count - 1
                    sp1.ActiveSheet.Cells(y    +    2,    x    +    1)    =
dt.Rows(y).Item(dt.Columns(x).Caption)
```

```vb
                Next
            Next


        Case "Multi Line Vertical"

            For x As Integer = 0 To dt.Columns.Count - 1
                sp1.ActiveSheet.Cells(x + 1, 1) = dt.Columns(x).Caption
            Next

            For y As Integer = 0 To dt.Rows.Count - 1
                For x As Integer = 0 To dt.Columns.Count - 1
                    sp1.ActiveSheet.Cells(x      +     1,      y      +      2)      =
dt.Rows(y).Item(dt.Columns(x).Caption)
                Next
            Next


        Case "Single Line Horizontal"


            For x As Integer = 0 To dt.Columns.Count - 1
                sp1.ActiveSheet.Cells(1, x + 1) = dt.Columns(x).Caption
            Next

            For y As Integer = 0 To dt.Rows.Count - 1
                For x As Integer = 0 To dt.Columns.Count - 1
                    sp1.ActiveSheet.Cells(y      +     2,      x      +      1)      =
dt.Rows(y).Item(dt.Columns(x).Caption)
                Next
                Exit For
            Next


        Case "Single Line Vertical"


            For x As Integer = 0 To dt.Columns.Count - 1
                sp1.ActiveSheet.Cells(x + 1, 1) = dt.Columns(x).Caption
            Next
```

```vb
        For y As Integer = 0 To dt.Rows.Count - 1
            For x As Integer = 0 To dt.Columns.Count - 1
                sp1.ActiveSheet.Cells(x    +    1,    y    +    2)    =
dt.Rows(y).Item(dt.Columns(x).Caption)
            Next
            Exit For
        Next


    End Select

    End Sub
```

Making the Spreadsheet using a DataTable work

Another set of routines:

Module1.Open_DAO_Recordset_Using_DBEngine("ODBC;Driver={Microsoft Access Driver (*.mdb)};dbq=G:\nwind.mdb;", "Select * from [Products]")
Module1.Create_DataTable_using_DAO_Recordset_Using_DBEngine("Multi Line Horizontal")

Now, depending on what view we want to create:

Orientation:

Multi Line Horizontal

Module1.do_DataTable_code_for_Spreadsheet (AxSpreadsheet1

, "Multi Line Horizontal")

Multi Line Vertical

Module1.do_DataTable_code_for_Spreadsheet(AxSpreadsheet1

, "Multi Line Vertical")

Single Line Horizontal

Module1.do_DataTable_code_for_Spreadsheet(AxSpreadsheet1
, "Single Line Horizontal")

Single Line Vertical

Module1.do_DataTable_code_for_Spreadsheet(AxSpreadsheet1
, "Single Line Vertical")

Working with the Spreadsheet using a DataView

Chapter Subtitle

Public Sub do_DataView_code_for_Spreadsheet(ByVal sp1 As AxMicrosoft.Office.Interop.Owc11.AxSpreadsheet, ByVal Orientation As String)

```
sp1.ActiveSheet.Cells.Clear()


Select Case Orientation


  Case "Multi Line Horizontal"


    For x As Integer = 0 To dv.Table.Columns.Count - 1
      sp1.ActiveSheet.Cells(1, x + 1) = dv.table.Columns(x).Caption
    Next

    For y As Integer = 0 To dv.Table.Rows.Count - 1
      For x As Integer = 0 To dv.Table.Columns.Count - 1
```

```
                    sp1.ActiveSheet.Cells(y        +        2,      x      +         1)          =
dv.table.Rows(y).Item(dv.table.Columns(x).Caption)
                Next
            Next


        Case "Multi Line Vertical"

            For x As Integer = 0 To dv.Table.Columns.Count - 1
                sp1.ActiveSheet.Cells(x + 1, 1) = dv.table.Columns(x).Caption
            Next

            For y As Integer = 0 To dv.Table.Rows.Count - 1
                For x As Integer = 0 To dv.Table.Columns.Count - 1
                    sp1.ActiveSheet.Cells(x        +        1,      y      +        2)          =
dv.table.Rows(y).Item(dv.table.Columns(x).Caption)
                Next
            Next


        Case "Single Line Horizontal"


            For x As Integer = 0 To dv.Table.Columns.Count - 1
                sp1.ActiveSheet.Cells(1, x + 1) = dv.table.Columns(x).Caption
            Next

            For y As Integer = 0 To dv.Table.Rows.Count - 1
                For x As Integer = 0 To dv.Table.Columns.Count - 1
                    sp1.ActiveSheet.Cells(y        +        2,      x      +         1)          =
dv.Table.Rows(y).Item(dv.Table.Columns(x).Caption)
                Next
                Exit For
            Next


        Case "Single Line Vertical"


            For x As Integer = 0 To dv.Table.Columns.Count - 1
```

```
            sp1.ActiveSheet.Cells(x + 1, 1) = dv.table.Columns(x).Caption
        Next

        For y As Integer = 0 To dv.Table.Rows.Count - 1
            For x As Integer = 0 To dv.Table.Columns.Count - 1
                sp1.ActiveSheet.Cells(x       +       1,       y       +       2)       =
dv.Table.Rows(y).Item(dv.Table.Columns(x).Caption)
            Next
            Exit For
        Next


    End Select

    End Sub


End Module
```

Making the Spreadsheet using a DataView work

Getting boring, yet? Okay, the routines for the DataView.

Module1.Open_DAO_Recordset_Using_DBEngine("ODBC;Driver={Microsoft Access Driver (*.mdb)};dbq=G:\nwind.mdb;", "Select * from [Products]")
Module1.Create_DataView_using_DAO_Recordset_Using_DBEngine("Multi Line Horizontal")

Now, depending on what view we want to create:

Orientation:

Multi Line Horizontal

Module1.do_DataView_code_for_Spreadsheet (AxSpreadsheet1

, "Multi Line Horizontal")

Multi Line Vertical

Module1.do_DataView_code_for_Spreadsheet(AxSpreadsheet1

, "Multi Line Vertical")

Single Line Horizontal

Module1.do_DataView_code_for_Spreadsheet(AxSpreadsheet1
, "Single Line Horizontal")

Single Line Vertical

Module1.do_DataView_code_for_Spreadsheet(AxSpreadsheet1
, "Single Line Vertical")

To summarize

This book is what I call a core book. That means that around 6 variations of this book is possible with only the recordset routine being changed out.

I'm telling you this because it is important for you to know in advance that unless you want to see the same routines in each book, I'm being honest here. Purchase the e-book or read it for free, Get the code that makes the book different.

Good luck and happy coding!